To the Vet

2

Who goes to the vet?

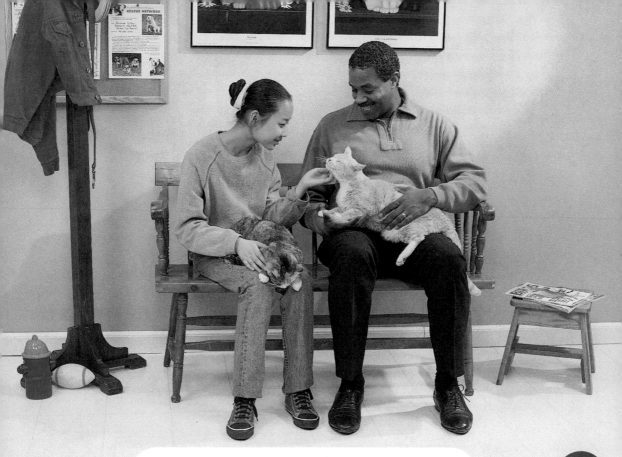

Cats go to the vet.

3

4

Dogs go to the vet.

Rabbits go to the vet.

5

6

Birds go to the vet.

Who goes to the vet?

Animals go to the vet.

GROOVY SATCHEL

Messenger-style satchels are great for school or for traveling to and from the office. Medium-weight cotton and linen-blend fabrics work well with this project. The pieced exterior is ideal for using fabrics from a coordinating bundle.

SKILL LEVEL: Intermediate

FINISHED BAG SIZE: approximately 12½" x 12" x 3"

TECHNIQUES:
- Lined Patch Pocket (page 13)
- Open-Ended Handle (page 15)
- Riveted Snaps (page 16)

MATERIALS

Yardage is based on 42"-wide fabric and 20"-wide interfacing.

½ yard of fabric A for outer bag and shoulder strap*

½ yard of fabric B for outer bag and upper panels*

½ yard of fabric C for gusset and flap

½ yard of fabric D for lining, gusset, and pocket*

2½ yards of fusible woven interfacing (Pellon SF101)**

⅞ yard of sew-in interfacing (Pellon 930)**

One ⅝" riveted snap

*If you are using directional prints, purchase ⅝ yard of each fabric and cut the pieces on the lengthwise grain.

**If you use 35½"-wide interfacing, purchase 1½ yards of the fusible woven interfacing (Vilene G700) and ⅝ yard of the sew-in (Vilene M12).

CUTTING

See "Good to Know" on page 57 for information on seam allowances and pattern pieces.

From fabric A, cut:
3 strips, 3½" x 19", for outer bag
2 strips, 4¾" x 19¾", for shoulder strap

From fabric B, cut:
2 strips, 3½" x 19", for outer bag
4 rectangles, 5" x 13½", for upper panels

From fabric C, cut:
2 gusset pieces
2 flap pieces

From fabric D, cut:
1 rectangle, 13½" x 19", for lining
2 gusset pieces
2 rectangles, 7" x 10", for pocket

Continued on page 57

"Groovy Satchel," made with fabric from the Boho collection by Urban Chicks for Moda Fabrics

Continued from page 55

From the fusible interfacing, cut:

5 strips, 3½" x 19", for outer bag

4 rectangles, 5" x 13½", for upper panels

4 gusset pieces

2 rectangles, 7" x 10", for interior pocket

2 strips, 4¾" x 19¾", for shoulder strap

2 flap pieces

From the sew-in interfacing, cut:

1 rectangle, 13½" x 19", for outer bag

1 flap piece

Contrasting gusset matches the flap.

> ### GOOD TO KNOW
>
> - All seam allowances are included in the pattern pieces and cutting instructions.
> - Seam allowances are ½" throughout, unless stated otherwise.
> - Use the Groovy Satchel gusset and flap patterns on pages 61 and 62.
> - Join the two pieces of the gusset pattern before cutting the fabrics.

PREPARATION

1 | Fuse the fusible interfacing pieces to the wrong side of the corresponding fabric pieces.

2 | Pin the sew-in interfacing to the wrong side of the corresponding lining. Baste ¼" from the edges.

3 | Transfer the markings from the gusset pattern to each fabric gusset.

PIECING THE OUTER BAG

1 | Stitch the 3½" x 19" strips of fabrics A and B together at the long edges, alternating their placement and using a ½" seam allowance.

2 | Press the seam allowances toward the fabric A strips and topstitch ¼" from the seams.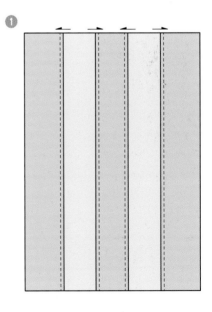

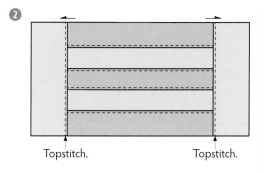

Topstitch.　　　　　Topstitch.

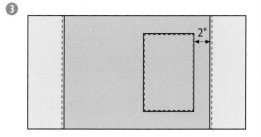

2"

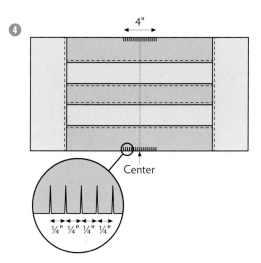

4"

Center

¼" ¼" ¼" ¼"

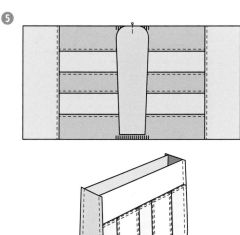

3 | With right sides together, sew an upper panel to each end of the pieced unit. If the fabric is a directional print, be sure both upper panels will appear right side up in the finished bag. Press the seam allowances toward the upper panels and topstitch ¼" from the seams. ❷

4 | Repeat step 3 to sew and topstitch the remaining upper panels to the ends of the lining piece.

POCKET

1 | Make the pocket, referring to "Lined Patch Pocket."

2 | With both pieces right side up, center the pocket on the lining piece with its top edge 2" below an upper panel. Stitch ⅛" from the sides and bottom edge of the pocket. ❸

GUSSETS

1 | Fold the outer bag in half to find the center (bottom) of the bag and mark the seam allowance on each side with a small clip. Be sure you don't clip through the seamline. Make an additional clip every ¼" for approximately 2" to each side of the center points. ❹

2 | With right sides together, place an outer gusset on one long edge of the outer bag, matching the center points, and pin. Continue aligning the side and bottom edges, easing the fabric around the curve of the gusset and up the sides of both pieces. Repeat to pin the second outer gusset to the other side of the outer bag.

3 | Stitch the gussets to the outer bag. ❺

4 | Notch the gusset curves and press the seam allowances open. Turn the bag right side out, smoothing the seams into position.

5 | Repeat steps 1–4 to join the gusset lining pieces to the bag lining, but leave the lining wrong side out.

SHOULDER STRAP

1 | Sew the two 4¾" x 19¾" strips of fabric A together at one short end, using a ⅜" seam allowance. Press the seam allowances open.

2 | Make the shoulder strap, referring to "Open-Ended Handle."

3 | Pin the ends of the shoulder strap to the outer bag between the marks on the upper edge of each gusset, matching the raw edges. Be sure that the strap is not twisted and baste ¼" from the raw edges. **6**

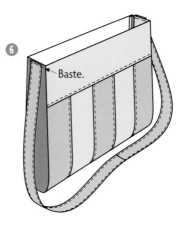

Baste.

BAG ASSEMBLY

1 | Insert the outer bag into the lining with right sides together, matching the gusset seams and aligning the top edges. You can place the lining with the pocket in the front or the back. Pin. Be sure that the shoulder strap is tucked out of the way between the layers. Stitch around the top edges, using a ⅜" seam allowance, leaving a 6" gap at the center front for turning. **7**

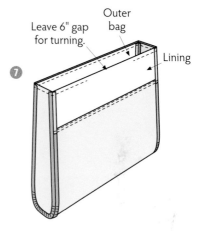

Leave 6" gap for turning.

Outer bag

Lining

2 | Turn the bag and lining right side out through the gap in the seam. Press both sections lightly, using a pressing cloth.

3 | Tuck the lining inside the outer bag and smooth it into place. Press the top edges so that the seam sits neatly at the top, pressing the shoulder strap away from the bag. Press the seam allowances along the gap to the wrong side and pin.

4 | Topstitch ¼" from the top edge of the bag, closing the gap as you stitch. **8**

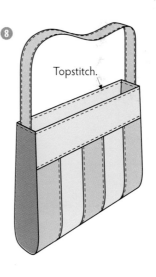

Topstitch.

FLAP

1 | Place the flap pieces right sides together and layer the sew-in interfacing on the bottom, aligning the sides and the bottom curved edges. Note that the interfacing is 1" shorter than the fabric pieces at the top edge. Pin the layers together.

2 | Stitch using a ⅜" seam allowance around all the edges, leaving a 5" gap at the center of the straight edge. Clip the curves and trim the corners diagonally. **9**

Leave 5" gap for turning.

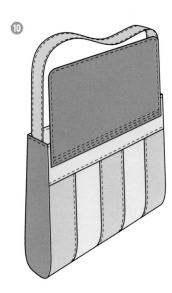

3 | Turn the flap right side out, smoothing the seams, corners, and curves into place, and press. Press the seam allowances along the gap to the wrong side and pin. Topstitch ¼" from all the edges, closing the gap as you stitch.

4 | With both pieces right side up, center the flap on the bag back with its straight edge 2" below the top edge of the bag and the majority of the flap extending beyond the bag edge. Pin securely, making sure the flap is positioned straight across the bag back.

5 | Topstitch the flap with a double row of stitching. Begin and end each line of stitches ¼" from the sides of the flap to avoid crossing the previous topstitches. Position the first row of topstitching ½" from the straight edge and the second row ¾" from the straight edge. ⑩

SNAP

Attach the top half of the snap to the flap closure, ½" from the bottom curved edge and centered from side to side. Fold the flap into its closed position and mark the corresponding placement for the snap on the bag front. Attach the bottom half of the snap at the mark. Refer to "Riveted Snaps" for more information.

A snap fastener finishes the bag.

> **KEEP IT FREE**
>
> If the pocket is on the lining front, be sure you fold it out of the way when attaching the snap through the bag front.

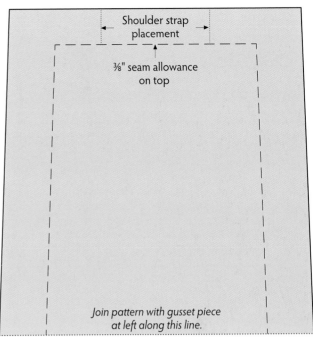

Shoulder strap placement

⅜" seam allowance on top

Join pattern with gusset piece at left along this line.

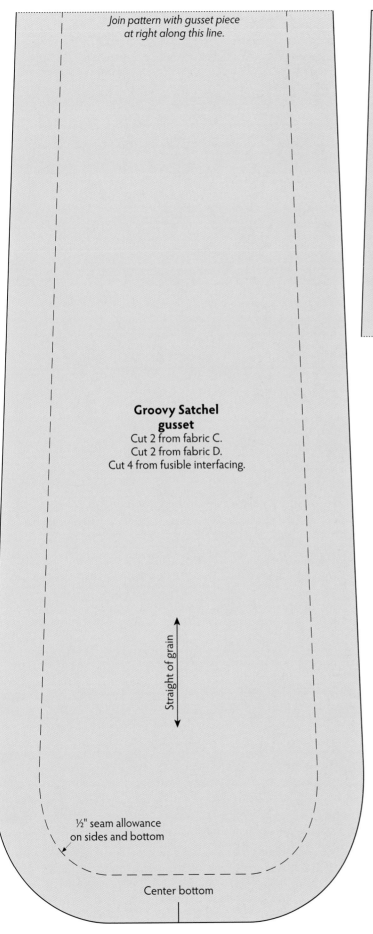

Join pattern with gusset piece at right along this line.

**Groovy Satchel
gusset**
Cut 2 from fabric C.
Cut 2 from fabric D.
Cut 4 from fusible interfacing.

Straight of grain

½" seam allowance
on sides and bottom

Center bottom

Cut sew-in interfacing to dotted line.

**Groovy Satchel
flap**
Cut 2 on fold from fabric C.
Cut 2 on fold from fusible interfacing.
Cut 1 on fold from sew-in interfacing.

Place on fold.

⅜" seam allowance

TRIANGLES TOTE

With an adjustable strap, this roomy tote can be worn on one shoulder or cross-body. The bag has an adjustable shoulder strap and a handy interior patch pocket.

SKILL LEVEL: Intermediate

FINISHED BAG SIZE: approximately 13¾" x 16"

TECHNIQUES:

- Lined Patch Pocket (page 13)
- Open-Ended Handle (page 15)
- Closed-End Handle (page 16)
- Riveted Snaps (page 16)

MATERIALS

Yardage is based on 42"-wide fabric and 20"-wide interfacings.

¾ yard of fabric A for outer bag, tabs, and shoulder strap

⅞ yard of fabric B for outer bag and lining

⅜ yard of fabric C for pocket and top bands

1¾ yards of fusible woven interfacing (Pellon SF101)*

⅞ yard of sew-in interfacing (Pellon 930)*

Two 1¼" metal D-rings

One 1½" metal adjustable slide

Two 1½" metal swivel hooks

One ⅝" riveted snap

If you use 35½"-wide interfacing, purchase 1 yard of the fusible woven interfacing (Vilene G700) and ½ yard of the sew-in (Vilene M12).

CUTTING

From fabric A, cut:

1 square, 16" x 16"; cut into quarters diagonally to yield
    4 triangles for outer bag

1 rectangle, 5" x 7", for tabs

1 strip, 6" x 42", for shoulder strap

From fabric B, cut:

1 square, 16" x 16"; cut into quarters diagonally to yield
    4 triangles for outer bag

2 squares, 14½" x 14½", for lining

From fabric C, cut:

2 squares, 10" x 10", for pocket

4 rectangles, 3" x 14½", for top bands

From the fusible interfacing, cut:

2 squares, 16" x 16"; cut into quarters diagonally to yield
    8 triangles for outer bag

1 square, 10" x 10", for pocket

4 rectangles, 3" x 14½", for top bands

1 strip, 3" x 35", for shoulder strap

From the sew-in interfacing, cut:

2 squares, 14½" x 14½", for lining

"Triangles Tote," made with fabric from the Sierra collection by Bren Talavera for Robert Kaufman Fabrics

PREPARATION

1 | Fuse the interfacing pieces to the corresponding triangles, top bands, and one pocket piece. Center the interfacing on the corresponding shoulder-strap fabric and fuse.

2 | Pin the sew-in interfacing to the lining pieces and baste ¼" from the edges.

OUTER BAG

1 | Pin and sew one A triangle to one B triangle along one of the short edges. Make four.

2 | Press the seam allowances toward the B triangles. Topstitch ¼" from the seams. ①

3 | Place two of the triangle units rights sides together, alternating the fabric placement. Match the seams and align the raw edges; pin. Stitch the long edge. Make two.

4 | Press the seam allowances open and topstitch each A triangle ¼" from the seam. Work from the center toward each corner, breaking the topstitching where the seamlines intersect.

5 | Trim the pieced units to measure 14½" x 14½". These are the outer-bag pieces. The B triangles are at the top and bottom. ②

TOP BANDS

1 | Stitch the bottom edge of a top band to the top edge of one outer-bag piece. Make two.

2 | Press the seam allowances toward the top bands and topstitch ¼" from the seam. ③

3 | Repeat steps 1 and 2 to join and topstitch the remaining top-band rectangles and the lining pieces.

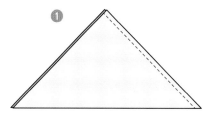

①

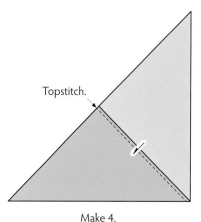

Topstitch.

Make 4.

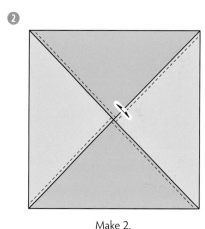

② Make 2.

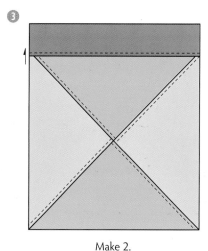

③ Make 2.

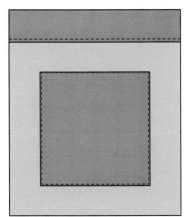

Topstitch.

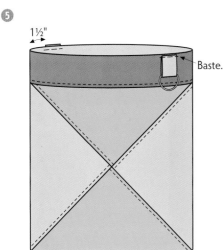

POCKET

1 | Make the interior pocket, referring to "Lined Patch Pocket."

2 | With both pieces right side up, center the pocket on one lining piece and pin. Topstitch ⅛" from the sides and bottom edge of the pocket. ❹

OUTER BAG AND LINING

1 | Pin the outer-bag units right sides together, matching the seamlines and aligning the raw edges. Stitch the sides and bottom edge.

2 | Trim the bottom corners diagonally and press the seam allowances open. Turn the bag right side out, smoothing the corners into place with a point turner. Press lightly, using a pressing cloth.

3 | Repeat steps 1 and 2 to sew the lining pieces together, but leave an 8" gap at the center bottom for turning. Leave the lining wrong side out.

D-RING TABS

1 | Refer to "Open-Ended Handle" to prepare the tab piece. Cut the tab in half widthwise to make two tabs of equal size.

2 | Thread a tab through a D-ring, folding the tab in half with the D-ring at the fold. Baste the raw edges together, ¼" from the edge. Make two.

3 | Pin one tab to the front of the outer bag, aligning the raw edges and positioning the tab 1½" from the bag's right-hand side seam. Baste in place, ¼" from the edge. Repeat to baste the other D-ring tab to the bag back, 1½" from the bag's left-hand side seam. ❺

BAG ASSEMBLY

1 | Insert the outer bag into the lining, right sides together. Match the side seams and align the top edges; pin. Be sure the D-ring tabs are tucked out of the way between the layers. Stitch the top edge.

2 | Turn the bag and lining right side out through the opening in the lining seam. Press both sections lightly using a pressing cloth. Press the seam allowances to the wrong side along the gap and pin. Stitch the gap closed, either by hand or with machine stitches placed close to the pressed edges.

3 | Tuck the lining inside the outer bag. Smooth it into place and press the top edges so that the seam sits neatly at the top, pressing the tabs away from the bag.

4 | Topstitch ¼" from the upper edge of the bag. **6**

5 | Attach the snap halves at the center of the top bands. Refer to "Riveted Snaps."

SHOULDER STRAP

1 | Make the shoulder strap, referring to "Closed-End Handle."

2 | Thread one end of the shoulder strap through the adjustable slide. Fold 1½" to the wrong side at the strap end and position the slide at the fold; pin. Topstitch near the strap end. Stitch again, ⅛" from the first line of stitches, to secure the strap end firmly. **7**

3 | Thread the other end of the strap through one of the swivel hooks. Pass the strap end back through the slide, creating a loop. **8**

4 | Thread the free end of the shoulder strap through the second swivel hook. Fold 1½" to the wrong side at the end of the strap and position the swivel hook in the fold; pin. Topstitch near the strap end. Stitch again, ⅛" from the first line of stitches, to secure the strap end firmly. **9**

5 | Snap the hooks onto the bag's D-rings.

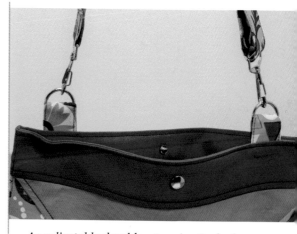

An adjustable shoulder strap is attached to the bag with swivel hooks and D-rings connected to offset tabs. A riveted snap provides the closure.

6
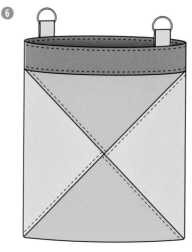

Topstitch.

7

8
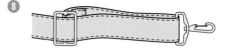

9
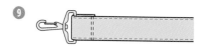

PURSE-FRAME CLUTCH

An elegant clutch is the perfect accessory for special events and evenings out. It also could be used as a pretty makeup bag. This project is suitable for medium-weight cottons and uses an 8" purse frame.

SKILL LEVEL: Intermediate

FINISHED PURSE SIZE: approximately 8" x 6½" x 2½"

TECHNIQUE: Boxed Bag Base (page 14)

MATERIALS

Yardage is based on 42"-wide fabric, 20"-wide interfacing, and 45"-wide fusible fleece.

⅜ yard of fabric A for outer bag

⅜ yard of fabric B for lining

¼ yard of fabric C for center panels

⅞ yard of fusible woven interfacing (Pellon SF101)*

⅜ yard of fusible fleece (Pellon 987F)*

Strong fabric glue

8" x 3" metal purse frame

24" length of ⅛"-diameter twisted paper cord or piping cord

Tool for inserting fabric and cord into purse frame (like an old pair of scissors or dinner knife)

*If you use 35½"-wide interfacing, purchase ⅝ yard of the fusible woven interfacing (Vilene G700) and ⅜ yard of the fusible fleece (Vilene H630).

CUTTING

See "Good to Know" on page 70 for information on seam allowances and pattern pieces.

From fabric A, cut:
2 main-bag pieces, for outer bag

From fabric B, cut:
2 main-bag pieces, for lining

From fabric C, cut:
2 rectangles, 5" x 9", for center panels

From the fusible interfacing, cut:
4 main-bag pieces, for outer bag and lining
2 rectangles, 4" x 9", for center panels

From the fusible fleece, cut:
2 main-bag pieces, for lining

"Purse-Frame Clutch," in an alternate colorway with a chain shoulder strap attached for versatility

"Purse-Frame Clutch," made with fabric from the PB&J collection by BasicGrey for Moda Fabrics. This clutch has a roomy interior for carrying essentials.

PREPARATION

1 | Fuse the interfacing pieces to the wrong side of the corresponding fabric pieces. Center the center-panel interfacing on the corresponding fabric before fusing.

2 | Center the fleece on the wrong side of the interfaced lining pieces and fuse. Use a pressing cloth to avoid melting the fleece.

3 | Transfer the dots from the pattern piece to the outer-bag and lining pieces.

CENTER PANELS

1 | Press ½" to the wrong side on each long edge of a center panel. Make two.

2 | With both pieces right side up, center a prepared panel on top of an outer bag. Match the top and bottom edges; pin. Topstitch ⅛" from the pressed edges. Make two. ❶

Topstitch.

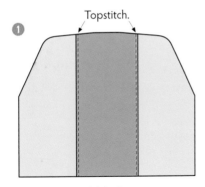

Make 2.

BAG UNITS

1 | Place the outer-bag units right sides together, matching the center-panel edges at the bottom. Pin.

2 | Stitch the sides and bottom seam, beginning and ending at the dots. Backstitch to reinforce the seam at the dots. Press the seam allowances open and leave the bag wrong side out. ❷

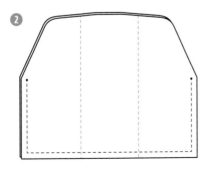

3 | Repeat steps 1 and 2 to stitch the lining pieces together, leaving a 4" gap at the center bottom for turning. Leave the lining wrong side out.

4 | Box the corners of the outer bag and lining to create a depth of 2½", referring to "Boxed Bag Base." Turn the outer bag right side out.

BAG ASSEMBLY

1 | Insert the outer bag into the lining with right sides together. Match the side seams and align the top edges, creating two flaps. Pin.

2 | Stitch the first flap from one side seam to the opposite side seam, between the dots, keeping the previous seam allowances out of the way. Backstitch at each end of the seam. Stitch the second flap in the same manner. Snip into the seam allowances on both sides of the side seams and notch the curved edges, being careful not to cut the stitches. ❸

3 | Turn the bag and lining right side out through the opening in the lining seam. Reach through the gap to smooth the flap edges into position.

4 | Press the seam allowances to the wrong side along the gap in the lining seam and pin. Stitch the gap closed, either by hand or with machine stitches placed close to the pressed edges.

5 | Tuck the lining into the bag and smooth into place. Press the top edges so that the seam sits neatly at the top. Topstitch ¼" from the edge of each upper flap, breaking the stitching at the side seams. ❹

PURSE FRAME

1 | Apply fabric glue into the channel on one side of the purse frame. Be sure the channel is fully coated with the glue. Let the glue sit for approximately five minutes so it becomes tacky.

2 | While waiting, measure and mark both flaps 1" from each side seam. Apply fabric glue carefully along the top edge of one flap only, from one marked position to the other. Allow the glue to sit until it becomes tacky.

Boxed corners for a flat bottom and depth

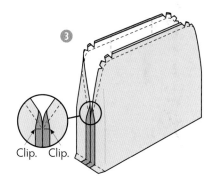

Clip.   Clip.

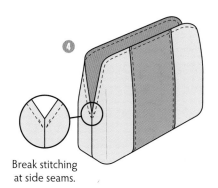

Break stitching at side seams.

The metal frame is stylish and secure.

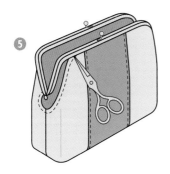

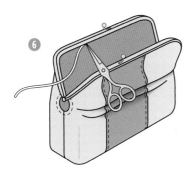

GLUE TIPS

- If you get some glue on the outside of the frame, it can be gently picked off when dry.
- Be careful to avoid glue on unintended fabric areas, as it's difficult to remove. To avoid spots, cover the fabric (both outer bag and lining) below the upper-edge topstitching with low-tack masking tape, leaving the top ¼" exposed.

3 | Working with the outer side of the purse facing you, position the top edge of the glued flap into the glued channel of the frame, matching the centers. Use a suitable tool to force the flap edges into the channel. Work your way into each curve and down each side, pushing the fabric edges firmly into the frame. Turn the purse around to the lining side, to push the edges in from that side as well. **5**

4 | Cut a 12" length of paper or piping cord and push it firmly into the frame's channel from the lining side of the purse, using the tool. This bulks up the edges within the channel, ensuring a tighter and stronger bond. Be sure the cord is pushed completely into the channel so that it can't be seen. If any excess cord remains at the end, snip it off. Let the purse sit for about 20 minutes before starting on the other flap. **6**

TIES THAT BOND

For an even stronger bond, coat the cord with fabric glue, letting it sit to become tacky before pushing the cord into the channel.

5 | Repeat steps 1–4 to insert the second purse flap into the other side of the purse frame. Let the purse sit overnight to dry and cure completely before using. If there is any glue on the metal frame, gently pick it off and polish the frame with a dry, soft cloth.

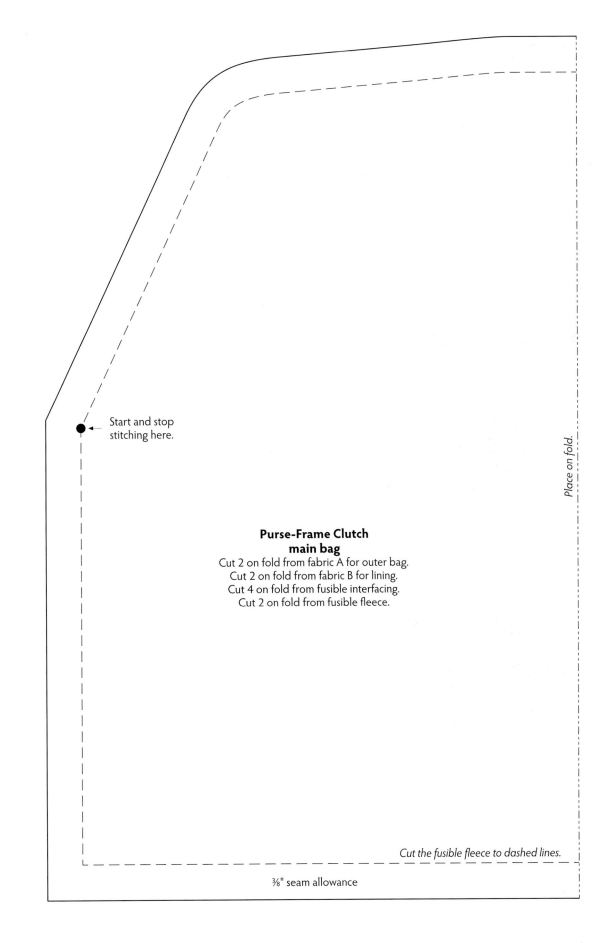

Start and stop
stitching here.

**Purse-Frame Clutch
main bag**
Cut 2 on fold from fabric A for outer bag.
Cut 2 on fold from fabric B for lining.
Cut 4 on fold from fusible interfacing.
Cut 2 on fold from fusible fleece.

Place on fold.

Cut the fusible fleece to dashed lines.

⅜" seam allowance

LAYERED SATCHEL

Make a modern satchel with coordinating medium-weight cottons. The layered exterior has great visual appeal, as well as making the bag strong and functional.

SKILL LEVEL: Intermediate

FINISHED BAG SIZE: approximately 13¼" x 14¼"

TECHNIQUES:

- Lined Patch Pocket (page 13)
- Open-Ended Handle (page 15)
- Closed-End Handle (page 16)

MATERIALS

Yardage is based on 42"-wide fabric and 20"-wide interfacing.

½ yard of fabric A for outer bag, flap, and pocket

¾ yard of fabric B for panel, tabs, upper bands, and shoulder strap

½ yard of fabric C for inner panels and lining

2 yards of fusible nonwoven interfacing (Pellon ES114)*

⅝ yard of sew-in interfacing (Pellon 930)*

Two 1¼" rectangular metal rings

Two ½" sew-on magnetic snaps

If you use 35½"-wide interfacing, purchase 1⅛ yards of the fusible nonwoven interfacing (Vilene F220) and ½ yard of the sew-in (Vilene M12).

CUTTING

See "Good to Know" on page 76 for information on seam allowances and pattern pieces.

From fabric A, cut:
1 rectangle, 14" x 18", for outer bag
2 flap pieces
2 rectangles, 7½" x 10", for pocket

From fabric B, cut:
1 rectangle, 8" x 18", for panel
1 rectangle, 5" x 7", for tabs
4 rectangles, 6" x 14", for upper bands
1 rectangle, 7" x 8", for flap panel
1 strip, 5" x 36", for shoulder strap

From fabric C, cut:
1 rectangle, 5" x 18", for inner panel
1 rectangle, 14" x 18", for lining
1 rectangle, 5" x 7", for flap inner panel

Continued on page 76

"Layered Satchel," made with fabric from the Wishes collection by Sweetwater for Moda Fabrics

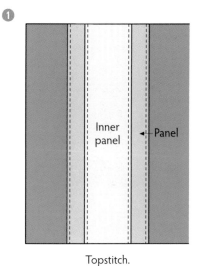

①

Inner panel ◄─|─► Panel

Topstitch.

②

Topstitch.

Continued from page 74

From the fusible interfacing, cut:
1 rectangle, 14" x 18", for outer bag
1 rectangle, 7" x 18", for panel
1 rectangle, 4" x 18", for inner panel
4 rectangles, 6" x 13", for upper bands
1 rectangle, 7½" x 10", for pocket
2 flap pieces
1 rectangle, 6" x 7", for flap panel
1 rectangle, 4" x 6", for flap inner panel
1 strip, 2½" x 31", for shoulder strap

From the sew-in interfacing, cut:
1 rectangle, 14" x 18", for lining
1 flap piece

GOOD TO KNOW

- All seam allowances are included in the pattern piece and cutting instructions.

- Seam allowances are ⅜" throughout, unless stated otherwise.

- For this project, I've used sew-on magnetic snaps, which are hand-sewn to the bag after construction. If you prefer to use standard magnetic snaps, you will need to install them during construction.

- Use the Layered Satchel flap pattern on page 80.

PREPARATION

1 | Fuse the interfacing pieces to the wrong side of the corresponding fabric pieces, centering any smaller interfacing pieces on the corresponding fabric before fusing.

2 | Pin the sew-in interfacing to the wrong side of the lining and one of the flap pieces, 1" from the straight edge. Baste ¼" from the outer edges, leaving the straight edge free.

OUTER BAG

1 | Press ½" to the wrong side on both long edges of the panel and inner panel. Center the panel on the outer bag, with both pieces right side up, and pin. Topstitch ¼" from both long edges.

2 | Center the inner panel on the fabric B panel, right side up, and pin. Topstitch ¼" from both long edges. **①**

3 | Sew the bottom edge of an upper band to one short edge of the outer bag. Sew a second upper band to the other short edge. If you're using a directional print, be sure it is oriented correctly.

4 | Press the seam allowances toward the upper bands. Topstitch the upper bands, ¼" from the seams. **②**

5 | Repeat steps 3 and 4 to sew and topstitch the remaining upper bands to the lining.

POCKET

1 | Make the pocket, referring to "Lined Patch Pocket."

2 | With both pieces right side up, center the pocket on the lining with the top edge of the pocket 1" from one of the upper bands. Stitch ⅛" from the sides and bottom edge of the pocket. **③**

OUTER BAG AND LINING

1 | With right sides together, fold the outer bag in half widthwise, matching the upper-band seams, and pin the side edges. Stitch the side seams. **④**

2 | Trim the bottom corners diagonally, being careful not to clip the stitching. Press the seam allowances open and turn the bag right side out, using a point turner to work the corners into place.

3 | Repeat steps 1 and 2 to fold and sew the lining, leaving a 6" gap in one side seam for turning. Leave the lining wrong side out. **⑤**

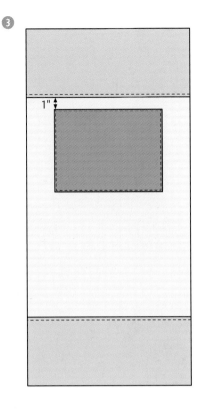

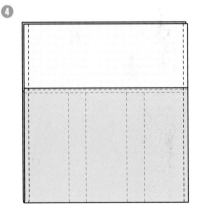

Leave 6" gap for turning.

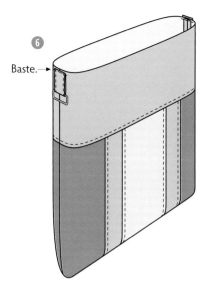

Baste.

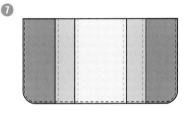

Topstitch.

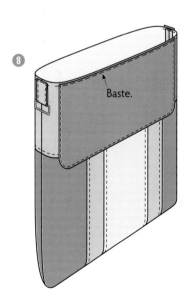

Baste.

TABS

1 | Refer to "Open-Ended Handle" to construct the tab piece. Cut the unit in half widthwise to make two tabs of equal size.

2 | Thread one tab through a rectangular ring, folding the tab in half with the ring at the fold. Baste the raw edges together, ¼" from the edge. Make two.

3 | Center a tab over one of the bag side seams, matching the raw edges, and pin. Baste the tab in place, ¼" from the bag's upper edge. Repeat to baste the second tab over the other side seam. **6**

FLAP

1 | Press ½" to the wrong side along the 7" edges of both flap panels.

2 | With both pieces right side up, center the panel on top of the flap piece without sew-in interfacing. Match the raw edges at the top and bottom and pin. Topstitch ¼" from the pressed edges of the panel.

3 | Center the inner panel on the fabric B panel, right side up, aligning the raw edges, and pin. Topstitch ¼" from both pressed edges of the inner panel.

4 | Place the two flaps right sides together and pin. Stitch the side and bottom edges, leaving the long straight edge open. Clip the curves and trim the seam allowances to a scant ¼".

5 | Turn the flap right side out, smoothing the seams and curves into place, and press, using a pressing cloth. Topstitch ⅛" from the side and bottom edges, leaving the long straight edge open. **7**

6 | With right sides together, center the flap on the back of the outer bag, matching the raw edges, and pin. Be sure the small spaces between the sides of the flap and the tabs are equal. Baste ¼" from the raw edge. **8**

BAG ASSEMBLY

1 | Insert the outer bag into the lining, right sides together. Match the side seams and align the top edges; pin. Be sure the tabs and flap are tucked out of the way between the layers. Stitch the top edge.

> ### LENGTHEN UP
> Increase the stitch length when sewing over the tabs and flap to cope with the thickness of multiple layers.

2 | Turn the bag and lining right side out through the gap in the lining seam. Press both sections lightly, using a pressing cloth. Press the seam allowances to the wrong side along the gap and pin. Stitch the gap closed, either by hand or with machine stitches placed close to the pressed edges.

3 | Tuck the lining into the bag and smooth it into place. Press the upper edge so that the seam sits neatly at the top, pressing the flap and tabs away from the bag. Topstitch ¼" from the upper edge. **9**

SHOULDER STRAP

1 | Make the shoulder strap, referring to "Closed-End Handle."

2 | Thread one end of the strap through one of the rectangular rings. Fold 1" of the strap to the wrong side, positioning the ring in the fold, and pin. Topstitch near the end of the strap and again, ⅛" from the first stitches, to secure the strap end. Repeat to attach the other end of the strap to the second rectangular ring. **10**

SNAPS

1 | Sew the magnetic parts of the two snaps to the front upper band of the bag, positioning each one ½" above the upper-band seam and centered on a visible section of the fabric B panel.

2 | Sew the nonmagnetic parts of the two snaps to the lining side of the flap, positioning each one ½" from the bottom edge of the flap and in line with the corresponding snap parts on the bag.

Dual snaps secure the wide flap

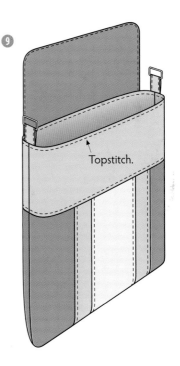

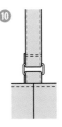

Cut sew-in interfacing to dotted line.

**Layered Satchel
flap**
Cut 2 on fold from fabric A.
Cut 2 on fold from fusible interfacing.
Cut 1 on fold from sew-in interfacing.

Place on fold.

⅜" seam allowance

PLEATED SHOULDER BAG

Very pretty and extremely practical, this shoulder bag is just the right size to carry lots of bits and pieces, without being too big. The adjustable strap allows you to change the handle length to suit your style.

SKILL LEVEL: Intermediate

FINISHED BAG SIZE: approximately 16" x 13", excluding strap

TECHNIQUES:

- Lined Patch Pocket (page 13)
- Closed-End Handle (page 16)
- Magnetic Snaps (page 17)

MATERIALS

Yardage is based on 42"-wide fabric and 20"-wide interfacing.

½ yard of fabric A for outer bag and shoulder strap

½ yard of fabric B for upper bag and pocket

⅜ yard of fabric C for lining

2¼ yards of fusible woven interfacing (Pellon SF101)*

Two 1" squares of fusible fleece (Pellon 987F) for snap reinforcement

One ¾" magnetic snap

Two 1¼" rectangular metal rings

One 1¼" metal adjustable slide

*If you use 35½"-wide interfacing, purchase 1⅛ yards of the fusible woven interfacing (Vilene G700).

CUTTING

See "Good to Know" on page 83 for information on seam allowances and pattern pieces.

From fabric A, cut:
2 rectangles, 10" x 17", for outer bag
1 strip, 5" x 42", for shoulder strap

From fabric B, cut:
4 upper-bag pieces
2 rectangles, 7" x 10", for pocket

From fabric C, cut:
2 lining pieces

From the fusible interfacing, cut:
2 rectangles, 10" x 17", for outer bag
2 lining pieces
4 upper-bag pieces
1 rectangle, 7" x 10", for pocket
1 strip, 2½" x 35", for shoulder strap

"Pleated Shoulder Bag," made with fabric from the Mid Century Modern collection for Michael Miller Fabrics

- All seam allowances are included in the pattern pieces and cutting instructions.
- Seam allowances are ⅜" throughout, unless stated otherwise.
- Use the Pleated Shoulder Bag upper-bag and lining patterns on pages 86 and 87.
- Join the two pieces of the lining pattern before cutting the fabrics.

PREPARATION

Fuse the interfacing pieces to the wrong side of the corresponding fabric pieces, centering the shoulder-strap interfacing on the corresponding fabric strip before fusing. There will be 2" without interfacing at the top of each upper-bag piece in the tab areas.

SNAP

1 | Transfer the snap placement mark from the pattern to the two upper-bag pieces that will be used on the bag interior.

2 | Referring to "Magnetic Snaps," attach the magnetic snap parts to the upper-bag pieces, using the 1" squares of fusible fleece as reinforcement.

PLEATS

1 | Measure and mark the top edge of each outer-bag piece 5" (A) and 3" (B) from the side edges.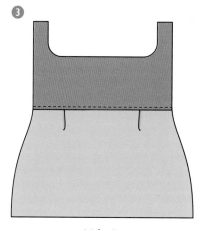

2 | Fold the fabric, wrong sides together, at one A position. Bring the fold to meet the nearest B, forming a pleat, and pin. Repeat with the A and B on the other side of the outer-bag piece. The pleated upper edge should measure 13"; adjust the folds if necessary and baste the pleats ¼" from the upper edge. Make two.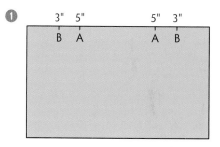

UPPER BAG

1 | Sew the bottom edge of an upper bag to the pleated edge of one outer-bag piece. Press the seam allowances toward the upper bag and topstitch ¼" from the seams. Make two.

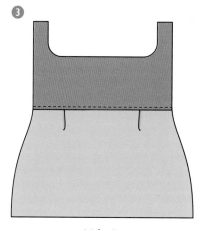

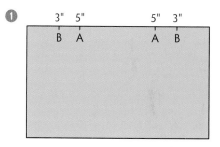

Make 2.

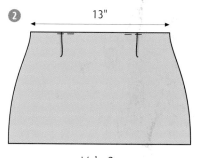

Make 2.

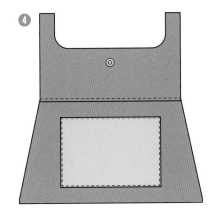

2 | Repeat step 1 to sew and topstitch the upper-bag pieces with snaps to the lining pieces.

POCKET

1 | Make the pocket, referring to "Lined Patch Pocket."

2 | With both pieces right side up, center the pocket on one lining piece and pin. Stitch ⅛" from the sides and bottom edge of the pocket. **④**

OUTER BAG AND LINING

1 | Place the outer-bag units right sides together, matching the horizontal seams, and pin. Stitch the sides and bottom edge.

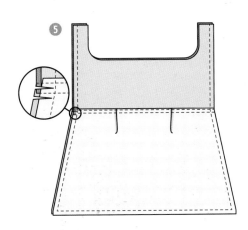

2 | Trim the bottom corners diagonally and clip the seam allowances on both sides of the upper-panel seam, being careful not to clip the stitching. Press the seam allowances open and turn the bag right side out. Use a point turner to work the corners into place. **⑤**

3 | Repeat steps 1 and 2 with the lining units, leaving a 6" gap at the center bottom for turning. Leave the lining wrong side out.

BAG ASSEMBLY

1 | Insert the outer bag into the lining, right sides together. Match the side seams and align the raw edges; pin. Stitch the top edge. Clip the curves and trim the corners diagonally. **⑥**

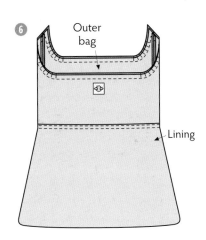

Outer bag

Lining

2 | Turn the bag and lining right side out through the opening in the lining seam. Reach through the gap and use a point turner to work the corners of the upper edge into place.

3 | Press the seam allowances to the wrong side along the opening in the lining and pin. Stitch the gap closed, either by hand or with machine stitches placed close to the pressed edges.

4 | Tuck the lining into the outer bag and smooth it into place. Press the top edges of the bag so that the seam sits neatly at the top. Topstitch ¼" from the upper edge of the bag. **⑦**

Topstitch.

RECTANGULAR RINGS

1 | Thread a rectangular ring onto one tab (narrow area) at the side of the bag's top edge. Fold 1" of the tab to the lining side and pin or baste.

2 | Topstitch along the end of the tab. Stitch again, ⅛" from the first line of stitching, to secure. Repeat to attach the second rectangular ring to the other side of the bag. **8**

THE THICK OF IT

When stitching the tab ends to the bag, increase the stitch length and use a sharp needle to cope with the thickness and multiple layers.

SHOULDER STRAP

1 | Make the shoulder strap, referring to "Closed-End Handle."

2 | Thread one end of the shoulder strap through the adjustable slide. Fold 1½" of the strap to the wrong side with the slide at the fold and pin. Topstitch along the end of the strap. Stitch again, ⅛" from the first line of stitching, to secure the strap end firmly. **9**

3 | Pass the other end of the strap through one rectangular ring. Weave it through the slide, creating a loop. **10**

4 | Thread the free end of the strap through the second rectangular ring. Be sure the strap is not twisted. Fold 1½" of the strap end to the wrong side and topstitch two parallel lines as before. **11**

An adjustable shoulder strap allows the option of wearing on one shoulder or cross body.

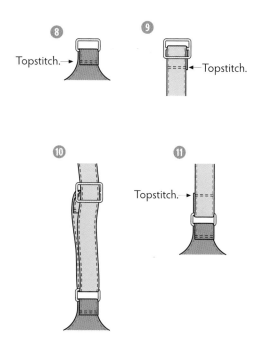

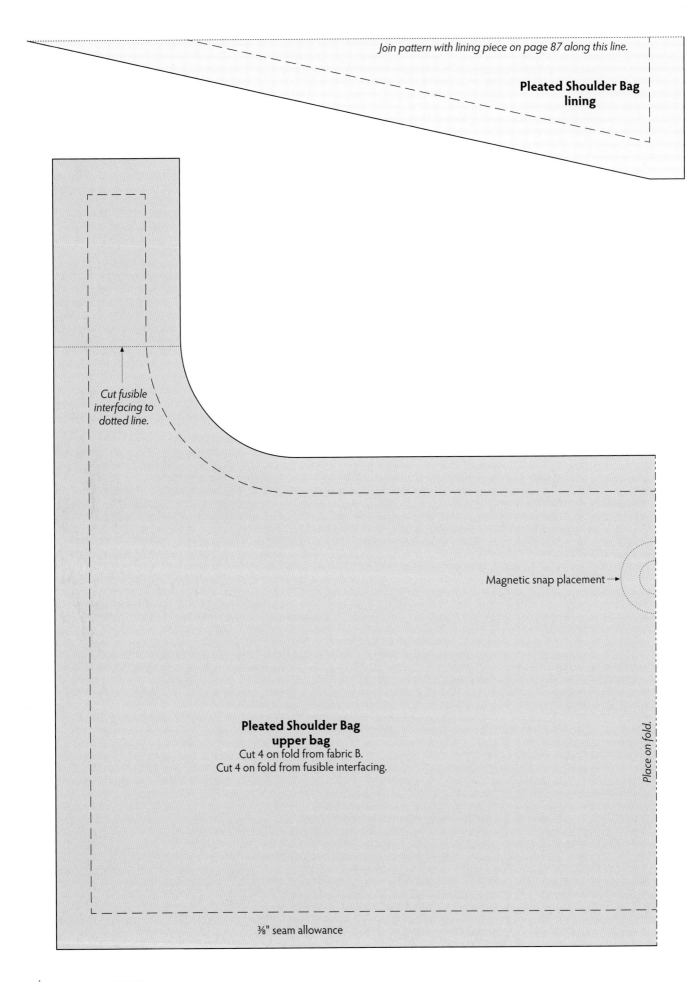

Join pattern with lining piece on page 87 along this line.

**Pleated Shoulder Bag
lining**

*Cut fusible
interfacing to
dotted line.*

Magnetic snap placement →

Place on fold.

**Pleated Shoulder Bag
upper bag**
Cut 4 on fold from fabric B.
Cut 4 on fold from fusible interfacing.

⅜" seam allowance

**Pleated Shoulder Bag
lining**
Cut 2 on fold from fabric C.
Cut 2 on fold from fusible interfacing.

Place on fold.

Join pattern with lining piece on page 86 along this line.

⅜" seam allowance

TRI-FOLD WALLET

Make a fabulous tri-fold wallet with scraps from your stash or a bundle of fat quarters to achieve your own unique designer look. The wallet includes pockets for credit cards, cash, and a small notepad or coupons, plus a zipped coin pocket.

SKILL LEVEL: Advanced

FINISHED WALLET SIZE: approximately 11¾" x 7" (open)

TECHNIQUE: Bordered Sew-In Pocket (page 14)

MATERIALS

Yardage is based on 42"-wide fabric, 20"-wide interfacing, and 45"-wide fusible fleece.

¼ yard of fabric A for exterior, pockets, and tab

¼ yard of fabric B for pockets and tab

¼ yard of fabric C for interior

½ yard of fusible woven interfacing (Pellon SF101)*

¼ yard of fusible fleece (Pellon 987F)*

7" zipper

2" length of 1"- or ¾"-wide Velcro

Air-soluble fabric marker or chalk soluble

Seam ripper

¼"-wide double-sided tape

Sewing clips (optional)

*If you use 35½"-wide interfacing, purchase ¼ yard of the fusible woven interfacing (Vilene G700) and ¼ yard of the fusible fleece (Vilene H630).

CUTTING

From fabric A, cut:
1 rectangle, 7⅞" x 12¾", for exterior
4 rectangles, 2⅜" x 4¾", for credit-card pockets
1 rectangle, 4¾" x 6¼", for notepad pocket
1 rectangle, 3½" x 7⅞", for cash pocket
1 rectangle, 3½" x 4¾", for tab

From fabric B, cut:
4 rectangles, 3½" x 4¾", for credit-card pocket linings
1 rectangle, 4¾" x 7⅞", for notepad pocket lining
1 rectangle, 5⅛" x 7⅞", for cash pocket lining
1 rectangle, 3½" x 4¾", for tab lining

From fabric C, cut:
3 rectangles, 4¾" x 7⅞", for interior
2 rectangles, 4" x 7⅛", for coin pocket

From the fusible interfacing, cut:
4 rectangles, 2" x 4", for credit-card pockets
1 rectangle, 4" x 5⅞", for notepad pocket
1 rectangle, 3⅛" x 7⅛", for cash pocket
2 rectangles, 3½" x 4¾", for tab
5 rectangles, 4" x 7⅛", for interior and coin pocket

From the fusible fleece, cut:
1 rectangle, 6⅝" x 11½", for exterior

"Tri-Fold Wallet," made with fabric from the Juggling Summer collection by Brigitte Heitland for Zen Chic, for Moda Fabrics

The wallet has plenty of interior pockets to hold credit cards, cash, and a small notepad.

PREPARATION

1 | Fuse the interfacing pieces to the wrong sides of the corresponding pocket pieces, aligning the top edges and centering the interfacing from side to side.

2 | Fuse the interfacing pieces to the wrong sides of the corresponding tab and coin-pocket pieces, matching the raw edges.

3 | Center the interfacing pieces on the wrong sides of the corresponding interior pieces and fuse.

4 | Center the fleece on the wrong side of the exterior and fuse. Use a pressing cloth to avoid melting the fleece.

MAKING AND ATTACHING THE POCKETS

1 | Make the credit-card, cash, and notepad pockets, referring to "Bordered Sew-In Pocket."

2 | Place an interior piece and one of the credit-card pockets right sides together, with the pocket's long raw edge 1⅞" above the bottom short edge of the interior piece. Pin and stitch ⅜" from the long raw edge of the pocket. ❶

3 | Repeat step 2 to attach the second credit-card pocket, positioning the long raw edge of the pocket 3" above the bottom edge of the interior piece.

4 | Repeat step 2 again with the third credit-card pocket, this time positioning the long raw edge of the pocket 4⅛" above the bottom edge of the interior piece. ❷

❶
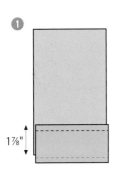
1⅞"

❷
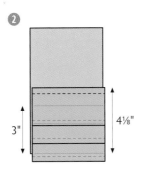
3"   4⅛"

5 | Fold each pocket upward, over the seam allowances, so that they lie flat against the interior piece. Press and pin.

6 | Lay the fourth credit-card pocket on the interior unit, right side up, matching the pocket's long raw edge to the bottom edge of the interior piece. Pin. Baste ¼" from the sides and bottom edge of the unit. ❸

7 | With both pieces right side up, place the notepad pocket on a second interior piece, aligning the sides and short bottom edges. Pin. Baste the pocket ¼" from the raw edges. ❹

8 | With both pieces right side up, place the cash pocket on top of the remaining interior piece. Align the long raw edge of the pocket to the right-hand edge of the interior piece and pin. Baste the pocket ¼" from the raw edges. ❺

ASSEMBLING THE INTERIOR

1 | Lay out the three interior units side by side, as shown at right. With right sides together, place the cash-pocket unit on the credit-card unit. Match the raw edges and pin, or use sewing clips to hold the pieces together. Stitch the units together. Open out the units and press the seam allowances toward the cash pocket.

2 | Stitch the notepad-pocket unit to the left side of the credit-card unit in the same way. Open out the units and press the seam allowances toward the notepad pocket.

3 | Using a pressing cloth, press the interior from the right side to ensure that everything is lying flat. ❻

MAKING THE COIN POCKET

1 | Sew the zipper tapes together just above the zipper pull, using a few hand stitches. Measure 6" from the start of the teeth and trim the zipper there. Stitch across the zipper teeth ⅜" from the trimmed end to make a new zipper stop. ❼

2 | Draw a 5½" x ⅜" rectangle on the wrong side of one coin-pocket piece, 1¼" from the top long edge and centered from side to side. Draw a line along the center of the rectangle, starting and stopping ¼" from the short ends. Draw a V from each end of the central line into the corners of the rectangle. ❽

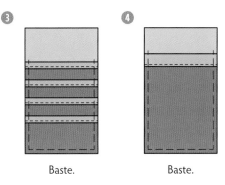

Baste. Baste.

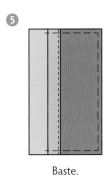

Baste.

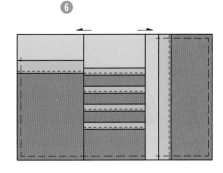

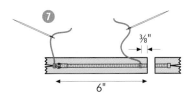

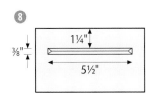

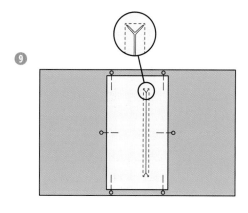

3 | Center the marked coin pocket on top of the exterior piece, right sides together, with the pocket's short edges parallel to the long edges of the exterior; pin. Stitch along the outer edge of the drawn rectangle through all the layers.

4 | Cut along the central line of the rectangle, cutting through all the layers. Snip into the corners along the Vs, clipping close to the corners but not through the stitches. **9**

> **SEAMS GREAT**
>
> Use a seam ripper to make a starting hole on the center line before continuing to clip with scissors.

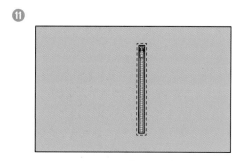

5 | Turn the coin-pocket edges through the opening so that the pieces are now wrong sides together. Press the opening from both sides to define and neaten it. **10**

6 | Apply double-sided tape to the right side of both zipper tapes. With both right side up, place the prepared exterior on top of the zipper, positioning the zipper neatly inside the opening. Apply pressure around the opening to secure the taped zipper edges to the fabric.

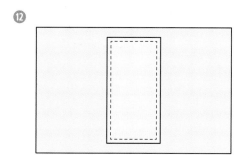

Topstitch around
the zipper opening.

7 | Topstitch ⅛" from all edges of the rectangular opening, using a zipper foot. **11**

8 | Place the second coin pocket on the first, right sides together and raw edges matched. Pin the pocket edges together, keeping the exterior out of the way as you pin. Stitch ½" from all four edges of the pocket, folding the exterior out of the way as you stitch. Trim the seam allowances to ¼". **12**

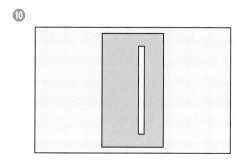

Stitch 2 pocket pieces together,
holding main body out of the way.

ATTACHING THE FASTENER

1 | Apply double-sided tape to the wrong side of one half of the Velcro fastener. Center the fastener on the right side of the exterior, ⅝" below the zipper opening, and press into place.

2 | Fold the coin pocket out of the way and pin so that it won't be caught in the stitching. Topstitch ⅛" from the edges of the Velcro fastener. ⑬

ASSEMBLING THE WALLET

1 | With the interior unit right side up, place the exterior unit on top, right sides together, with the Velcro fastener to the left of the zipper. Align the raw edges and pin the layers together, or use sewing clips. Stitch both long edges and the short edge nearest the notepad pocket. Leave the short edge nearest the cash pocket open. ⑭

2 | Trim the stitched corners diagonally and turn the wallet right side out, smoothing the corners and seams neatly into place. Press the edges, using a pressing cloth.

3 | Fold ½" to the wrong side along the raw edges and press. Hold the folded edges in place with sewing clips or pins. ⑮

TOPSTITCHING THE POCKET SECTIONS

1 | Pin the layers of the wallet together, or use sewing clips around the edges.

2 | Topstitch in the ditch along each seam between pocket sections. Topstitch ⅜" to the right of the seam joining the cash pocket to the rest of the wallet.

> ### COLOR MATTERS
>
> To blend the topstitching in on both sides of the wallet, use a needle thread that matches the interior and a bobbin thread that matches the exterior fabric.

⑬

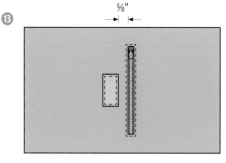

⅝"

Fold pocket out of the way when topstitching Velcro in place.

⑭

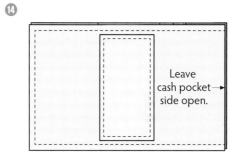

Leave cash pocket side open.

⑮

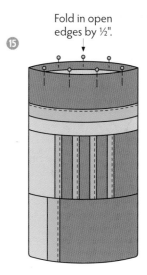

Fold in open edges by ½".

An exterior zipped pocket is perfect for storing coins. A tab closure wraps around the wallet, keeping everything secure.

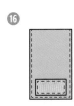

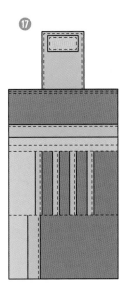

MAKING THE TAB

1 | Place the tab pieces right sides together and stitch, leaving the short bottom edge open. Trim the stitched corners diagonally.

2 | Turn the tab right side out, gently working the corners and seams into place, and press. Topstitch approximately ⅛" from the three stitched edges, leaving the open edge unstitched.

3 | Stitch the other half of the Velcro fastener to the lining side of the tab, centering it ¼" from the short stitched edge. **16**

FINISHING THE WALLET

1 | Insert ¾" of the tab's open end into the open end of the wallet, with the tab lining on the same side as wallet interior. Pin.

2 | Match the pressed edges of the wallet around the tab, ensuring that the pressed edges are aligned through the tab. Pin or clip the edges together, or baste by hand if preferred.

THE LINEUP

To be sure the pressed edges are aligned on both sides of the tab, stick a pin straight through the wallet from the exterior to the interior. Adjust the edges if necessary.

3 | Topstitch ⅛" from the wallet opening to close the wallet and secure the tab. Topstitch again, ¼" from the edge. **17**

THROUGH THE THICKNESS

The layers will add up to quite a thickness when you're stitching the wallet opening. Use a new sharp needle and a longer stitch to cope with the thickness.

4 | To close the wallet, first fold the notepad section to the interior and press along the fold. Next, fold the cash pocket into place and press. Bring the tab around the wallet and fasten into place.

Acknowledgments

I think this might be like giving a speech for winning an Oscar! I have so many people to thank, and I really do feel as if I've won some major prize.

First, my deepest thanks go to my family, who have always supported me in my many crafting ventures and continually helped me to believe in myself. Allan, kids, Mum, Dad, Karen, and Jemma, you all mean the world to me. Thank you.

To Julie Briggs, editor of *Sewing World* magazine, I owe special thanks. The opportunity you gave me, to be a contributor for your wonderful magazine, is what really started me on this journey. It never ceases to fill my heart with pride when I see my work in the magazine. Thank you!

To Fiona Pullen of www.thesewingdirectory. co.uk, I'd like to say a big thank-you. Your support, friendliness, and unending devotion to what you do are very inspiring. I wish you the very best with your new craft-business book too!

I was very lucky to receive some fantastic fabric and interfacing, which I've used in some of the projects. Thank you to Michele Stang from Pellon, Chris Taylor from Vilene, Debbie Outlaw from Moda Fabrics, Teresa Coates from Robert Kaufman Fabrics, Christine Osmers from Michael Miller Fabrics, and Elizabeth West from EQS, the UK distributor for Michael Miller Fabrics.

Special thanks to the entire team at Martingale for turning my dream into a reality and for producing this beautiful book.

Lastly, a huge thanks to my blog followers and customers. The lovely comments, support, advice, and friendliness that you have all shown me over the years have been amazing. What a wonderful crafting community we have. I hope you know that you have all played a big part in giving me the confidence to do this.

Thank you to all,

~ *Susan*

RESOURCES

My favorite manufacturers and suppliers of fabric, interfacing, and bag-making hardware are:

FABRIC COMPANIES

Art Gallery Fabrics
www.artgalleryfabrics.com

Michael Miller Fabrics
www.michaelmillerfabrics.com

Moda Fabrics
www.unitednotions.com

Robert Kaufman Fabrics
www.robertkaufman.com

UK Distributor for Michael Miller Fabrics
www.eqsuk.com

FABRIC RETAILERS

www.eclecticmaker.co.uk
www.etsy.com/shop/fabricshoppe
www.etsy.com/shop/fancypantsfabric
www.etsy.com/shop/stitchinstash
www.misformake.co.uk
www.plushaddict.co.uk

INTERFACING

www.pellonprojects.com
www.susieddesigns.co.uk
www.vilene-retail.com

BAG-MAKING HARDWARE

www.buckleguy.com
www.susieddesigns.co.uk

About the Author

SUSAN lives in Scotland with her husband and four children. Having enjoyed a variety of crafts since childhood, she launched her sewing business SusieDDesigns in 2012, designing and creating modern bags, accessories, and associated sewing patterns. Susan shares her patterns on Etsy and Craftsy as well as her own website, www.susieddesigns.co.uk. She also writes a blog at http://susieddesigns.wordpress.com.

Susan's bag-making projects and articles are regularly published in *Sewing World* magazine, to which she's contributed since 2012. Her creations have been featured on the front cover of the magazine on numerous occasions. She's also been a regular contributor to *Love Sewing* magazine since 2014.